Slide

Slide

Barbara Myers

Carolyn Marie Souaid, Editor

Signature
EDITIONS

Cover design by Lesley Mather, JeleDesign.
Photo of Barbara Myers by Lesley Mather.

This book was printed on Ancient Forest Friendly paper.
Printed and bound in Canada by Marquis Book Printing Inc.

We acknowledge the support of The Canada Council for the Arts and the Manitoba Arts Council for our publishing program.

ACKNOWLEDGEMENTS

Some of these poems were previously published in periodicals and anthologies, including the *Literary Review of Canada*, *Arc Poetry Magazine*, *The New Quarterly*, *Other Voices*, *Bywords*, *Amethyst Review*, and/or anthologized in *In Fine Form, The Canadian Book of Form Poetry*, *Soundings*, *Body Language*, and a number of Cranberry Tree Press annual collections, as well as in locally-produced anthologies. Thanks to all the editors. Generous readers who reviewed early versions of poems include Sylvia Adams, Diana Brebner, John B Lee, Rhea Tregebov, Gary Geddes, and Don Domanski; Steven Heighton read a portion more recently, and Elise Partridge provided thoughtful comments on most of the poems in the collection. I am deeply indebted to them all. Thanks to Roz Rubenstein for her gimlet eye in copyediting. Thanks to my daughter Lesley Mather (JeleDesign) for designing the stunning cover. I appreciate beyond words the love and support of a large family, and the encouragement that comes from being part of a vital/viral community of poetry friends. I also thank Anne H., and a special thank you goes to Judy — sister, critic, best friend. The financial support of the Ontario Arts Council Writers' Reserve, and the City of Ottawa arts funding, and study bursaries from the Banff School of Fine Arts and the University of New Brunswick's Maritime Writers' Workshop are all gratefully acknowledged, as are awards from the Scarborough Arts Council, *Other Voices*, the *Grist Mill*, *People's Poetry Letter*, and *Arc Poetry Magazine*. And thank you to Carolyn Marie Souaid who edited this book for Signature with a very discerning eye.

Library and Archives Canada Cataloguing in Publication

Myers, Barbara J. (Barbara Jean)
Slide / Barbara Myers.

Poems.
ISBN 978-1-897109-34-2

I. Title.

PS8626.Y36S55 2009 C813'.6 C2009-904905-8

Signature Editions
P.O. Box 206, RPO Corydon, Winnipeg, Manitoba, R3M 3S7
www.signature-editions.com

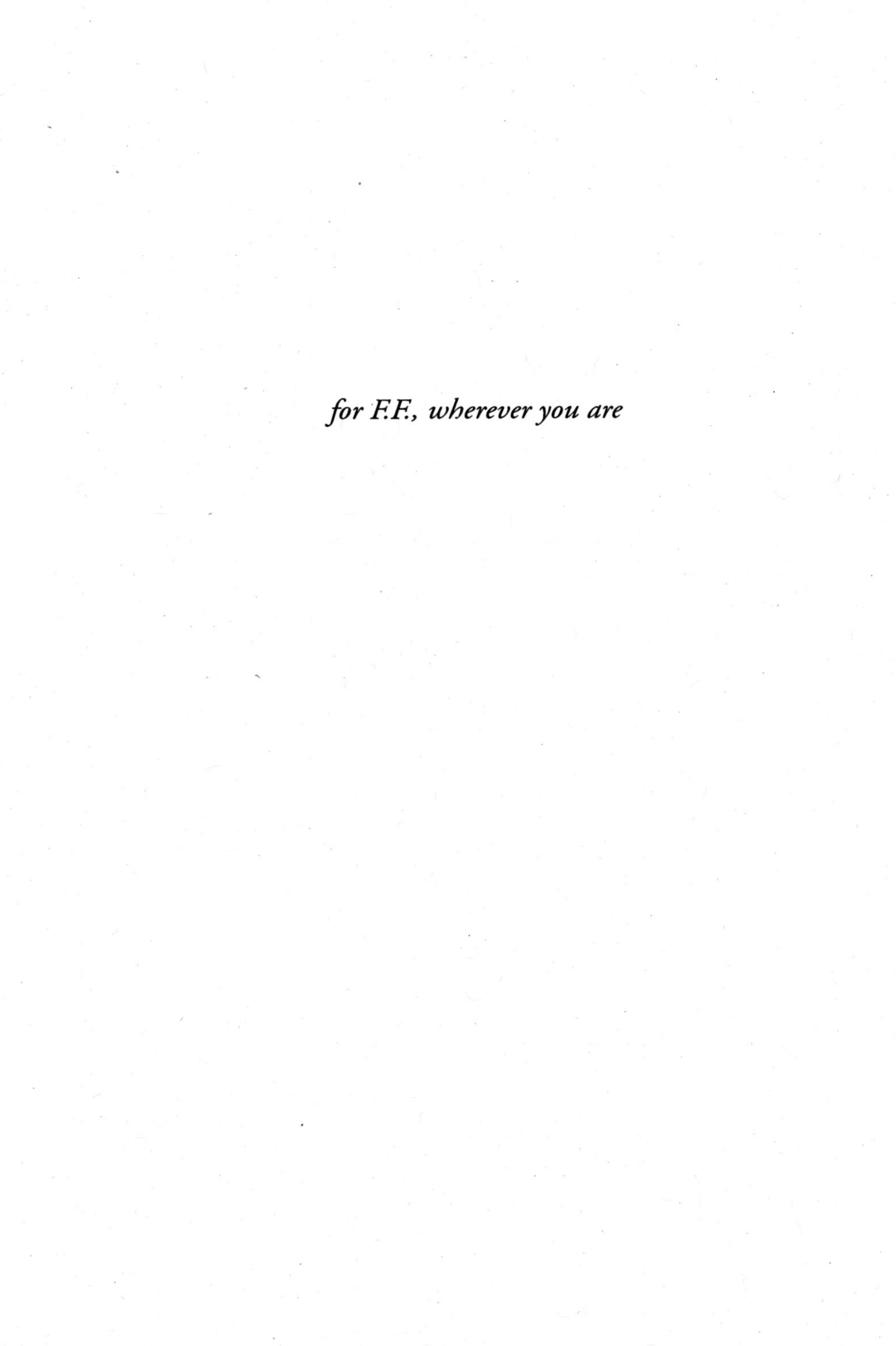

for F.F., wherever you are

Contents

Instructions for the Era of Water

Tiger Lilies

The Scattered Congregation

Instructions for the Era of Water

Because human life is transient, all manner of figures are woven into its fabric.
— Shundo Aoyama, *Zen Seeds*

Instructions for the Era of Water

— after Tomas Tranströmer

The sea has taken its place leaning against the wall
It is like a petition to the land
It is full of memory

Allow the sea to enter the land
Accept the energy of water, its fullness
Have no hidden plans for draining

Let the field become a lake
for ultimate survival
The man who stuck his finger in the dyke
now pulls it out
The river channel will drown
her past

Let there be floating settlements
amphibious houses not on stilts
but floating, floating

Let water be
the new land

turn its face to us
invite our return.

Wash of the Moon

1.

Closing on midnight
a full hammered-brass moon
mottled cloud cover.
From the frosty sidewalk we look south by south-east
not to miss the Leonid meteor shower
show of the century —

now and then a bright flash, the sky
like that screen in the test of peripheral vision:
press a button when a pinpoint flares;
the same question, do you see
what's there or do your eyes play tricks
register false positives,

as though streaking comet debris
could help you understand the finite mysteries
of this earth you stand on, other bodies in space,
seen and unseen, surrounding the clump of matter
you call *yourself*

all seemingly present at the same moment
rushing (not purposely to end, although you will,
leaving others behind as you blink out)
try for a better look
before dawn, when the clouds are thinner
the wash of the moon less bright.

2.

remember is a rubbery word
for this knowing by heart
when, called or not called,
the god is present

in the smell, the sound, the sight
you were there
and where you were
returns — bidden or not bidden
your past peppered
with desert islands you wash up upon
again and again, imposing
their dimensions, their hollow *proofs*.

You call them or more often they call you
sweep in, take you like a lover
unexpected, the more muscular
for needing no invocation

until one day you turn your back
determine to clean house
throw them out, the clutter of them
their tedious insistence —
dependents who keep you from attending
to fresh ephemera:

sky dust, earth dust,
the near shore, its wildlife
where, if the Buddha were to point to a flower
you would be the one to smile, say *ah!*

You Meet Her

You meet her again, by chance;
it is Wednesday. Chance does not mean
this meeting was not foreordained
or that Wednesdays are auspicious.

She is going to work, serious
in her red coat (blood requires oxygen,
this colour does not breathe).
She steps over wet paving blocks

in her thin black shoes,
but do not think because it is raining
that fecundity or rebirth occur
or that she is weeping at your return.

Sorrow has escaped from her veins
like fog rising off a salty sea. She agrees
to have coffee, even though her feet are wet,
only because she has forgotten

the vocabulary you taught her.
You invent signs for *miss you*
but she springs away, laughing, for a bus
to a foreign country:

note that laughter may not signify
her true state of mind.

Constellation

> The idea of separation
> unleashes its luminous line
> — Charles Wright

So long and narrow
all length no breadth

the ***x*** axis, time's unbroken arrow
birth to death, life to life, you are here

at the intersection sliced by ***y***, as above
so below, common and mysterious,

as if you could really know where you are

except in relation to objects on a grid,
lines running as if parallel

or joining the dots in this winter
constellation, Great Nebula in Orion.

Whose line is it anyway? Should we let it in?
What can we do except make things up

test them for roadworthiness, see if
Cartesian coordinates live up to their promise, guide

us to the same truck stop at the same time
while the coffee's still fresh and hot

and the jukebox's playing.

Ice Fog

We live in an old chaos of the sun
— Wallace Stevens

Night thickens with ice fog — an off-white
Arctic gustiness along slickening streets;
yellow headlights beam short/long codes

just beyond the bounds of deciphering;
snow begins its wildly soft accumulation.
A small animal stumbles out of hiding

ill and weak, weaving further distortion
—where in this tapestry is the bridge,
where the river? An act is pulling itself together —

large objects collect and mass in the distance,
language is bent like spoons by practiced minds
a studied calm preliminary.

A person — a woman, although it could
be a man — navigates through snow
hands tight upon the steering wheel

blindsided by wasted starry nights
failures that pockmark the skin —
wrong turns in better light.

Dream Prison

Power failure. Waking, you try the switches,
push them. Nothing. Rooms remain dark, their edges
blurred and dreaming. You're the one dreaming. Wake now,
crumpled-up sleeper.

See your body curled on the bed, insensate,
morning's call a light-bringing far-off praying.
Sleep-imprisoned powerless mortal being,
why do you struggle?

Harvest

They have cracked the code for corn
and here is an artist's illustration in glinting gold
curling taut as ribbon pulled across a scissors blade

mirabile dictu, DNA instructions for life.
In the cornfields brown male tassels
swing like sporran on a kilt, pollen spent

harvest ready. I comb my fingers through
rough stamens, tug at tight leaf
covers, expose glistening rows of cream-yellow

flesh mounding like tiny young breasts
scantily wrapped in silk, indelicately robust.
I read about what agri-business has forced,

planted deeper than the worm used to burrow
a calculated code (adulterous intimacy)
to armour ancient grain against invaders,

moved it, just like that, across an alien threshold,
exiled from its kin: *genus preposterous.*
Opposing winds stir up the fields, new

generations of Ruth pray for a plague, a havoc
of saviour locusts to descend, break the foreign code
fill the impostors with worms.

Selene

> In the various phases of her person...Marilyn Monroe is a manifestation of the White Goddess herself... [News Report, 1960]

There is nothing between me and my flesh
but the moon: my full white breasts, my belly,
my swellings and shadowy recesses

(*...bright Selene, having bathed her beautiful skin*
in the Ocean, puts on her shining raiment...)

It's important that we speak
I know your tongue, even when you refuse mine.

I do this for you, for love of you — for your love.
Fifty children
perhaps a hundred, my gift to Endymion.
Shhh! They are sleeping,
waiting for me, their mother, their wife.

Many times I have neared that shore but you
are not through with me, roughly waken me
so long as there is light in my flesh.
Listen closely... love this body
even as night comes, try to be steady.
It is never too much. It is always too much.

Consider the salmon
how their flashing skins leave the ocean
dark with memory.

I am with you only a little while
a rip tide in my wake.

Light Writing

for Marilyn Monroe

In the beginning she came in full colour,
arcs of red blue green radiance
a rainbow blooming from a raindrop's
reflected light, a circle centred
on the anti-solar point
directly opposite the sun.

Camera began as camera obscura
in a dark room, pinhole of light
where Renaissance artists traced
inverted reflections of the outside world,
taught themselves depth of field.

Through years of tinkering with silver salts,
gluey collodion, fumes of mercury,
images captured and held,
negatives reversed to positives
recording with perfect
fidelity in the constant lover's
shuttering ground glass eye,

it came to this:

how she peeled it all off
in an agony of trust

a laughing girl on a beach
exposed in a bathing suit.

Call of the Wild

At home in bush untrampled on
away from shadows cities cast
he drives his truck to hell and gone.

His life's been one long marathon
he struggles to outwit his past
strikes out for bush untrampled on.

He can't take heart from tonsured lawn
craves a wilder seed outcast
and drives his truck to hell and gone —

for the lake, at twilight, any season,
rough bark, and burrows hidden fast
of homes in bush untrampled on.

Just to be there with fern and fawn,
under unbuilt sky — even dark with cloud,
he drives his truck to hell and gone.

Connected to a self beyond
disguised in nature, safe at last,
to be home in bush untrampled on
he drives his truck to hell and gone.

Summer Exercises On the Ottawa River

(August, 2006)

By beach and floating dock, fire pit and volleyball net
yawning kids feed on peach-plum cobbler, draw elaborate graffiti
while we take coffee, sleep-deprived by last night's blasts and explosions:

across the river in Petawawa vigorous post-teens train in the dark
a hundred here, a hundred there—for firefights and reconstruction
in the country Alexander the Great couldn't tame.

At the cottage we watch live telecasts of dead soldiers
slow-marched in their coffins on their buddies' shoulders;
like giant beetles, flag-draped carapaces on sightless legs.

Here where we holiday, sounds carry across the river:
Petawawa's soldiers rehearsing manoeuvres,
simulating IEDs, Kandahar, counter-insurgency.

We practise horseshoe toss, take careless morning swims
uneasy in the frame where soldiers risk returning slow
on borrowed legs. Beetles, most ancient and abundant order.

Against A Grand Unified

Never mind how life began on earth or what
dark matter is composed of
just tell me, what is this
elderly cat thinking

this clockwork orange-and-white
who goes to a favourite spot then
changes her mind and curls up
someplace else

purrs when I pet her but wouldn't turn a hair
if I disappeared.
Before a dark window
I wonder at the starry sky,

she bats at specks on the glass
to tease them before
she eats them, unruffled
by the theorist's cat-in-a-box

and the urge to explain
in terms of quantum physics
that nothing happens
until you look.

Film Noir

Late November afternoon
bus along a country road,
the sky a gangster
in a dark suit.

Across the field a village's
trembling lights
hold for dear life.
Who sets bread and wine
on the table, then
clears it away?

Headlamps hit the road,
the bus's inverse
shadow going on
ahead, her shade
gathering speed.

Form

Love, that loosener of limbs, now shakes me again.
— Sappho

All that's bendable of the body
toes, hips, elbows, knees,
becomes hyperflexible
the beginning of meltdown
heated out-of-shapeness
an impulse to dissolve
to be absorbed...

I watch as you sleep
discovering essence
in the unguarded body,
the crooked elbow,
bent knee,
the bones of your head
curved like knight's armour.

Impossible to speak of the body
without speaking of love,
and you, gathered in stillness
a sleep promising waking,

or to know why I should find your brow
so noble, a sculpted shield,
while I sit watching,
loose in so many places.

I Ching Trees

They have the gift, these free
tree spirits throwing their shadows
on the pillowing snow,

horizontal hieroglyphs
languorously reaching and stretching,
released from cramped

tree verticality,
cast like I Ching sticks
blue-black trigrams

trunk lines crossed with branch
lines on the whitened-out park,
Books of Revelation

for those who can read.
Earth turns in the eye
of the sun, shadows

shift. I throw in my lot
with the trees, my lengthening shadow
pulses, confounding prophecy

as if the Sun's burning instruction
were neither here nor there.
As if I were not snow-blind.

Labyrinth Moon

Winter solstice moon, blind magnet, mirrors
black ice, gilds raw bones of trees.

All day she examines what they had in common:
the river, the ancient hills, the bridge.

We hardly know ourselves what would make us happy—
how can he blame her for his empty days?

Rescuers say the world of lost people is suffused
with sameness. Blind running. Looking without seeing.

Here in this labyrinth, a curved geometry
leads the way to a perfect circle at the centre.

Stop looking for significance! You think events
conspire when really so much is accidental.

The South Pole, with its waves of ice and staggering
emptiness, was the most perfect home she had ever found.

Thoughts scatter like mice. Oh my dear cousin,
there is more than one way to be lost.

Body / Nobody

> Who has availed to read the causes of things,
> who has knowledge of the woodland gods?
> — Virgil

Rainy day in Santa Fe, gallery of sun-dried bricks,
wooden floors, stone women breathing on sturdy children.

Works of art "always let you down,"
Bruce Chatwin said. What did he need?

You are counting out your days of two-breastedness
preparing in your unbelief for fire and knives.

Even at night, there is no need to stumble — ghostly
light cushions the edges of tables and chairs.

The first time happens only once: turn a corner and see
the Winged Victory of Samothrace, alighting.

If you want to know, the secret of you is also the secret of me;
there are no therefores among the children.

In an upstairs room a wrinkled wizard screens the new film
of his life's work, chides his apprentice for careless living.

Before Turning the Corner

Before turning the corner, one ritual wave.
Impatient for my old ways, I am leaving you again.

The Milky Way swathes the forest sky above the railway line:
winter solstice; transverse planets; Capricorn reigns.

Do you yearn to issue commands? Stay! Stay here!
Pain moves to pleasure, pleasure to pain.

Remember the stars somewhere around Charlo,
our blunt fingers groping the fabric even as it frays.

This train moves too fast, ice melts in praise or censure.
Your fragrance on my pillow: what we lose, oh what we gain.

For the Roar

sometimes you take your bland
exterior to a coffee shop
just for the roar

cappuccino frothing/ice scooping/
    rock music heavy on drums/
        20 simultaneous conversations

you stand at construction sites
the pounding shrieking groove
scraping out holes, powering them up floor over floor,

the lure of violent crashing

letting the noise speak
your heart's clamouring

Salt Dreams

Salt dreams of childhood, wet brine solutions
crystals crusting wet-dry coasts —

the envy of solid substances because
it dissolves, lost in the other yet intact.

O salt of bread, of cucumbers and cured fish,
salt of blood, of tears, of placental cells,

of little girls with their bare belly buttons
the too-salty little girls pretending out in the rain,

O curve of the atmosphere's thinning membrane
there are those too young

for rims around a margarita sunset,
seawater ions that go too far too soon

Black Umbrellas — *nunc stans*

Waiting in wet dust
for the bus in the rain
        its squishy wheels

thunderstorms light us and roll on by
a festival of black umbrellas crosses
into Parliament Hill

where crews hammer platforms, loop wires,
a week before summer spectacles.

Just behind my eyes, the same trees
are decked with coloured lights in early dusk,
hearten heaps of rounded snow.

This is life gathering speed
gathering seasons into the eternal now

where unexpected lilacs hang
heavy over the sidewalk,

take me high on a wood-and-rope
swing in the weedy old backyard.

Equilibrium

Glory be to God for dappled things
for tamarack's blue silhouette
wavering on a pleasured wall
            lace's patterned intermittence
                        leaf and twig that bruise
a still-drawn bedroom window shade

holding the soft middle ground of
in-between, the way clouds and twilight
cut sun's tough brilliancy, the way
            your lover kisses curve of throat
                        before imprecision vanishes
and he becomes so sharply

drawn his profile bites clear into day.
The shade flies up against your eye
ruins this pause, night's equinox —
            but in belief earth will repeat
                        with sun her artful balance,
the shuddering bed tucks itself in.

The Medici Princess

Under glass the little princess
doesn't eat, drink, or go
to sleep. No air invades
with its busy chemistry.

The collector has arranged
pretty blocks and shiny
stars just so — the red ball
within reach of her slender

fingers, the royal amulet
and chains far less lovely
than the flesh they rest upon.
His meticulous blue lines

score the glass, vertically
bifurcate crown
to groin: lines traverse her
child's eyes side to side

like shutters; frame her
soft mouth in perpetuity.
His collection box holds
both treasure and adventure —

a map drawer tantalizingly
ajar, his princess in suspension
deathlessly awaiting
their happy-ever-after.

Q.E.D.

He smiles with all his teeth
capped better-than-ever after old football
smash-ups, bridging a gapped and broken leer:

I picked up your spoor years ago
when you crossed my path —
we were meant to come together

He means he smelled me subliminally
his sixth sense receptors
vibrating to my pheromones, those odourless

chemicals secreted through skin
picked up by his vomeronasal
organ and zapped by his hypothalamus

according to scientists
who want to prove such things exist.
They have already claimed sounds

beyond our hearing, colours outside
our rainbow spectrum, so why
should there not be chemicals in our sweat

specific to our species
the taste and smell of heaven
in a chunky ex-linebacker?

Fugue in Winter

These days colours are muted but everything speaks to me
sons and daughters grown gentle with each other in ritual reunions
pigeons that purr on the balcony like itinerant cats
                                                            making the circuit

everything speaks to me, winter relents
grown sons and daughters gentle with each other
a white complexion of mind
glow of shorn boughs in moonlight

winter relents everything speaks
long limbs of pearled boughs and bushes
generations of roses in this wrinkled berry
the colour of their voices gentle.

Tiger Lilies

How else to know our common root but through you
who are compost now on the Atlantic shelf?
— Maxine Kumin
from"Gladly"

Slide

The image clings to painted plaster
walls   reprised and magnified
35 mm laughs and poses larger than life
lean on the veranda
in casual immortality

a hale and profane granddad wipes
the mouth organ
a young flirtatious woman looks back
over her shoulder —
a galaxy of light sheddings, inconstant
scatterings of children in neat shorts

where's the grammar
for this — this was you, wasn't it

still and dark when the imaging light goes out
sliding back   into
your spine, your blood,
always the same age
they ever   you ever
were

Silver Cross Mother at the War Memorial on Remembrance Day

It feels strange to be here now, so many years after it all happened
I never left home before and it's many years ago I retired
from cleaning offices every blessed night, washing, waxing, polishing
same as I did ever since his father died, him still a baby, but
he was going to take care of it soon as he got back
his last letter so creased you can't read what it says but I know
every word, soon be over, soon be home.
I don't really know why I came today
although it was nice of you to pay my way and say I was to stand up
for all the mothers whose boys went over and didn't come back
as though we were brave to do it but we never had anything
to say about it and we're not sure what it means to be brave anyway —
here with all these statues around, these things that look like
they're out of some storybook, supposed to make us remember, I guess,
as though we could ever forget
but we don't remember it this way. What we remember
is uniforms and kitbags, and before that school bags
and cowlicks and toothaches, even to the day of birthing.
You think mothers are proud of their sons' sacrifices
but we always say to them be careful
us mothers are the ones that stop fights before they get out of hand.
To us, war is stupid
everyone all fired up to fix insults or pay back for bullying
and I don't really want no part of it, so thank you
but don't say I was brave because my son went to help out,
if I could have kept him home, I would have,
and when they sent the telegram and the sympathy
I heard the one word *killed.*
Don't say we're brave
say we grieve, say we sorrow,
say our sons were taken from us
and that every day we live, we wish it wasn't so.

Home, Again

Be the soft matter within this train's
hard shell, carried to receptive ground
whole as an eyeball. Some
of these trees weren't born when you left
but the seeds were on their way, certain
compositions of dust and water, intermittent light.

This is the way to the peninsula — wet light
in satin mud flats; the saltwater bay trains
a narrow neck of land to your certain
destination — you know it even as bare ground,
reddened winter branches, worn hills left
low on an eastern horizon. Bring some

red and yellow roses to where your people lie, some
baby pink carnations, the colour that lights
the pale skin of old mothers — flowers from a hothouse left
petal-soft on cold sod, blooms that are trained
to blossom just to be cut; put them to ground
again, even though killing frosts come soon and certain.

Be the blinking shutter, collecting frames of certain
welcome — now yours is the senior generation, some
— if not all — failing somewhere, maladies grounded
in joints or blood. The wonder is what lights
recognition still, what essence trains
an embodied current through features left

flabby or gaunt — it's still unique, what's left
This is the way the young inherit certainty:
as you shed it, skin by skin. Reboard the train,
moving again, the way you mean to move, some

things happening, keeping track or not, lighter
as you go, still drawn to the red-brown ground

you came from, whether or not they're grounds
for happiness. It's immaterial where you came in or left,

whether the story goes in a straight line, in dark or light.
You seem to be returning but it's uncertain,
isn't it? The tracks could go anywhere: some
are straight, some curve, and on them rides — or not — your train.

This is you: the red-brown ground, the speeding train.
Observe what's left. From possible ways, choose some.
It finds you, the light, it does. You're almost certain.

After Graduation

She spreads her blue skirt halfway down the hill
facing away from homes in pastel blocks;
in one a woman is preparing fish—
chowder or fishcakes with mustard pickles.

The girl on the hill studies the shadows
made by short tufted grasses, semaphores
waving like subdued prayer flags then stilled.
Pointing past her. At the woman cooking.

Across the road a yard of old graves waits
for dark, when it will rustle, and lovers
who walk the paths might lie between old stones.
Might draw in one breath. Might decide.

Percy's Remains

> The poem of the mind in the act of finding
> What will suffice.
> — Wallace Stevens

Times while driving, my brain is tapped like a xylophone,
rings out coffee. meadow flowers. a dusty closet.
No rhyme or reason.
What does tea signify as it rings in around middle C,
or blossoms that chime a common
chord—and what about stifled dustiness?

Today the smell of hot cedar planks, fragrant low cello notes
leave me wondering what my grandfather
might have had for breakfast in 1920, days when
he crept out of the house early to go fishing on the Dartmouth lakes
or the Shubenacadie River — his diary records only where he went
who was there, what the catch was, and — oh yes — the weather.

Would there have been a pot of oatmeal on the stove, or did he
grab bread and an apple from a bin in the cellar — if apples
lasted into spring. Thermos of tea, not coffee. Exactly a year
before he died of pneumonia, exposure, he wrote: *a regular deluge,*
wind to a gale. Tried to fish at mouth of West Brook
but could not cast a line owing to wind. At 2 pm started to walk

home; got a lift in from the lower end of Tap-Rail Lake
by J. Boyle with his automobile. He had a Mr Wilcox
of the Church of England with him who prescribed hot rum
as prevention against cold — not a dry stitch on our bodies.
I see him bringing home trout, perch, salmon, ordering
his experience like a poet, endowing his world with meaning

teaching his six-year-old: *Jim's first trip after trout, used his new rod.*
They say he knew all the trees and wildflowers of the eastern seaboard.
Years before, courting Christie, he sent her a picture postcard
of a fair-haired Edwardian beauty: *You are the sweetest girl I know.*
1909. Unsigned. Dusty now, on the way to crumbling
leaving only essences: apple blossoms, cedar. Morse's tea.

The Beginning of Melt

I heard you, mourning dove, today at dawn —

This time last year in March
a clock tolled the hour with sounds of birds —
yours came at seven,
cups of coffee gone cold,
small breakfasts —
light blankets on the big chair:
a mother dying.

Today, a mist-swathed sun backlights
the lateness of the season, sketched
in soft pencil: depressions
in the snow; two men and a boy
drill a hole in the distant river,
something big for bait stuck
on the end of a fishing line.

In the trees between here and there
flashes of blue and white, of grey;
winter jeered along by raucous caws
chick-a-dee-dee-dees,
plaintive phoebe, her seeds still buried.

Here this morning, your motherly
tan-and-cream body roosts on the sunny
bird feeder, pigeony breast spilling over the roof;
alert to the unseen crow, your
low coo-oo-oo-ing still pitched
in the register of grief,
even though you birds know melting,
and ice, you know, has had its day.

Fifteen

This is the jeep commandeered by the dashing uncle
with his major's pips and Van Johnson smile
splashing over the riverbed at low water

and this the river of learning to swim,
cousins up from the Boston States
teasing the dirt road bordered with wild roses;

Les Paul and Mary Ford, sliding guitar
and voice reverberating in overdub:
Dear One the World is Waiting for the Sunrise.

This is the Bedford Consolidated High School
dance, red-haired Myron unenticed by White Rain
hair conditioner, pedal pushers and pin curls

and this the Rifle Range the summer of living in an army hut,
Father in Japan sending thick letters home, his clear careful
handwriting; pictures of smiley people who called him *papasan;*

the radio at home tuned to *The Sandman* on CJCH,
singing with Eddie Fisher "Oh My Pa-Pa"
and going for rides on the jeep without doors.

Hazel

A horsey face, they said of her, mildly unkind,
the plump ones with their well-used wombs
that summer in 1949 at Fletcher's Lake.

A blue-eyed weed on a tough straight stalk,
she got cross when the children played Old Maid,
stuck to her beauty routine of cold cream

splashes of cold water, standing in the bushes
with a basin she'd dipped into the lake, keeping
well back to avoid the leeches, on holiday

from Lawton's Drugs where she minded cash,
from shopping and cooking for old parents, from
stepping in as practical nurse for quarantined nieces —

but at Fletcher's Lake everyone was on holiday
pies made with today's blueberry picking,
a homemade hammock and Reader's

Digest Condensed Books, evenings on the verandah
men playing cribbage and smoking their pipes
even the women peaceful and easy.

I could go back there now, wrap my nine-year-old
head in a flowered turban, shuffle the cards
and tell her fortune: *Yes, you will marry*

but many years from now and he will not make
you happy; you will travel a thousand miles,
you will live a long life and when you're gone

everyone will wish they had cherished you more.
But wait — let the fortune-teller have the power
to change her aunt's fate, find her a loving partner,

right there and then — give them long years
as the kind of couple who finish each other's sentences,
and joke about how irritating that is.

Tiger Lilies

He has such serious eyes, she says,
after he comes bringing crocuses
in January, and dozens of pictures.

This grandson left home years ago
unable to find something to live for
in the mindlessness of malls—

reckless as one who only worried about
how wild animals survive the winter.
Now, shiny shoulder-length hair

pulled into a ponytail, clean plaid
shirt sleeves over arms covered in tattoos,
he shows his grandmother pictures:

his laughing daughter, his wife
in clown suit at the country school,
an old dog and a puppy, the view

from where the picture window will be
in the house he's building, grey-blue
shades of the Rockies in the distance.

He sits close to hold her attention,
and so she can hear. This picture,
he says, I just turned a corner

and there they were— a bunch
of tiger lilies— they would have bloomed
whether I came or not, the woods

are like that. They do not speak
of the reason for his long trip east,
winter now so hard upon her.

February

> Who can leap the world's ties
> And sit with me among the white clouds?
> — Han-Shan

Footsteps crunching the snow
past my open window, the sound of singing.

Succumbing to heaviness, rooted things seize
gravity's full stop. I hold my falling

at arm's length, a schooled tension, never
to give in. But don't fruit ripen for the inevitable,

litter orchard floors under the snow?
Penetrate to the core, the hollow at the centre

of the apple, the space where seeds accumulate
heavier than an infant's trust

in lift — before the first shock
of refusing arms. The grace of a body

letting go, buoyancy of descent —
tight pointed seeds built for burrowing,

the swelling centre of a thousand apple blossoms.

To lay aside every weight, the effort to lift,
to know all motion comes as grace.

Baptism — February, 2003

— for Kyleigh

The young priest's satin vestment, blue
with turquoise lining, forms a cross
over outstretched arms, straight-leg
jeans, this ham-fisted young priest who
holds you tipped upside down over a basin,
dropping water over your forehead, you

won't remember; or that while you sob
later at the back of the church, your father
walking you back and forth, the red
blue and green stained glass mosaics
of saints dim in the storm clouds
and snow-thickening air, as the priest

a chevron of goatee under his lower lip,
tells the people he's just back
from a holiday in Cuba, its people so poor
they must share even their cars,
not so fortunate as we,
gathered in this comfortable church, our private

cars tethered at the curb, being snowed upon
as folk guitarists sing out parts of the Mass
and men and women go up to the altar to read —
your little part over quickly, too quickly perhaps
for us to see the full scope of you
in your white christening gown, your

wide-mouthed smiles, your tears,
as the young priest offers prayers for the armed
forces massing in Iraq, blesses wafers of bread
and the wine, and some of the people lining up
to take Communion see you nearly asleep now,
light settling and unsettling in your radius

on this snowy February afternoon
while surely many of us pray

for no war at all, no sides to choose,
as we leave in our ones and twos and threes
in warm coats, preparing to use long-handled brushes
on the snow amassing on our separate cars.

Sunyata

Warm summer wind, you should know
who I am, you carried me here
you who send sailboats
skimming the bay, arrange oboe and bassoon
duets in the lilting air.

I remember fragrances like that from my childhood
my mother and her sisters laughing in the lilac garden
at nothing at all, breathing form
into shirts and socks
hung out to dry.
        Their gusts blessed the billowing clothes, entered
        narrow tree worms dropping on invisible threads
        permeated the cells of skinny girls taking turns
        on a homemade swing.

Net curtains, starched and blued
stretched on racks
like first threads strung on a loom
requisite background
for random filaments,
the warp and woof of days to come.
        I see the sisters advance along the line
        aprons full of stiff wooden pegs
        wrung-out clothes in a tin tub
        brought like soft household gods
        into the sun.

The vision fills me with elation
and a kind of mutable courage,
waking on a breezy warm morning
knowing it will be a good day for drying.

Aunt Tango

A tango (like a marriage) is something you have to dance to the end.
— Anne Carson

Upending cups, spinning them
on their saucers you read the leaves

find in the wet residue patterns: a donkey
wait for a better time a broom *a new home.*

In the old conversation between solids and liquids
one unending stream floods your wrists

the little bones and hinges of your fingers,
vortices of no escape.

Incense masks the dank drains in your old home,
blinds and curtains drawn against migraines —

pure wool skirts and Burberry coats
wait in narrow closets for possible occasions.

You teach us the unrelenting tango, crushing
our hard ripening to your ribs and soft breasts,

our pressed-together feet sweep a figure eight
Jalousie! Stop. Turn. Sweep.

Your elegant ankles and wrists are willing.
Your long fingers stretch in a green continuing.

Constancy of Ephemera

an occasional table, occasion unknown
its purpose to hold something —
a chinese lamp with pearlized shade
porcelain ladies in crinolined skirts
a pot of bright chrysanthemums

the shine on wood from years
of beeswax infused with lavender
buffed and polished, an era
come and gone, leaving the shine behind
like a fading inspiration

as caring for what comes to you opens
a passage, and a gingerly dusting
can become a caress, stroking off particles
that smudge what the cabinetmaker had in mind:
a small table to hold a lamp and some yellow flowers.

Preservation

The air in the room is full of artificial
things, bought and sold in exhalations, candied ginger
in a jar on the table, a gingery stretched-out cat
where sun rolls over floor and furniture.

Outside, wind sweeps snow across
a hill, through toothpick trees, like desert sand
sifting east in sun-glinted gusts—today
Aesop's coat would not come off.

Shine of ice preserves what it does not kill,
invades the room through glass —
the cat's fur glistens where it rises in the magnetic air
bright as any particle of snow.

The Day The Telegram

(1945)

Only a boy knocking,
from his hands the black-bordered envelope
swooping in before they could think
filling the trembling rooms

with its dark raucous cawing
fading the green life from the potted fern
the rosy swirls from the stiff brocade
shrouding lamps and windows.

Only words on paper
took the house captive
stilled kitchen clatter, the levity
of our small racing feet, sent

our mothers silent to the kettle.
The message breathed absence
from a foreign sky where he'd floated
harnessed to silk, the bullets rising to greet him

his unguided body listing
into the tangled Rhineland forest.

Wasn't It Hot for June

— for L.E.R. (1914 – 1984)

Wasn't it hot for June
when the tall ships put into Halifax Harbour
          poignant as songs
                    silent as biers?

Safe and sound
out of rough water
their masts made the sign of the cross
against a too-blue sky
          steady in a wind
          blowing coy and soft
                    teasing for sail
                                        and the open sea.

Still waters smelling of salt and fish
deep cold waters gave them rest
in the temporary way of harbours everywhere
until   one heat heavy day
          in slow
          procession,
the wind having picked up (drawing breath for a dirge)
they sailed away
taking you with them
          winding out their sheets like strangers

and the harbour waters took up their hulls'
displacement   without a sign
that they were ever there
          moored
          upright
                    shining   in the sunlight

The Weight of Snow

A snowflake, a blizzard of one, weightless, entered your room.
— Mark Strand

Don't count on its coming back, that blizzard of one.
The snowflake rested for a moment on your armchair —
did you see its cathedral prisms, hear a monkish
plainsong evanescing to the sea?

Its praise, contagious, was your invitation.
I tell you this, partly to remind myself of snowflakes,
that for all their scandalous variety, their wisdom
is not cumulative. There, in your yellow chair

shards of sun along the floor, you
cross your ankles and read your book,
content to let your attention melt as though
one day, the sky could open and send each one

anew: you, the chair, the sun, your book
and I could call you, Mother, anytime,
see you lift your head and look at me
unconcerned about the weight of snow.

Westphal Poetry and Dance

It's a long time since the Westphal
Poetry and Dance Society
met in the corner bungalow
our first house,

babies sleeping safe in our hilarity,
lines about trees like charcoal tracings
giving way to free-form grand jetés
as we entertained our friends,

Mantovani's lush strings their excuse
(and mine) for impromptu dancing,
filigree patterns from a swag lamp
swaying on dark green walls.

Your wit straddled the line, enticed
by play but needing ironic distance —
funny how we slept so well as each
encroaching moment waltzed those lives away.

Now I only hear the major bulletins:
you're living in London, planning a trip to
Kenya — the cancer has returned. Our babies
now grown, wide awake, alarmed by the quiet.

I'll write you a poem for old times' sake,
take you by the hand and swing you around
the parquet floor —
it's 1965 in a Dartmouth suburb

you pick up a pencil and pretend
to take the minutes
just to make us laugh.

The End of the World

When everyone dies, that will be
the end of the world, you say
matter-of-factly, the woven orange
rope hammock pressing its pattern

of diamonds in your five-year-old thighs.
But how can everyone die, I say,
when there will always be
new babies born? You consider,

lime-green cotton cloche over dark
tangles. (Ancestral aunts and grandmothers
keep to their darkened rooms,
stilled with knowledge.)

The babies will die, too, you say
firmly, rocking the hammock so that
both you and your baby brother spill,
laughing, on the grass, clambering

up again and again to the wobbly
knotted fabric, tied between beech trees.

The Scattered Congregation

We got ready and showed our home
— Tomas Tranströmer

Heaven's Gate 1997

Still laced with rubble
from its messy cosmic birthing,
the comet seems to hover
just above the northern tree line.

I am driving home by starlight,
displaced, the hard bright angles of the city
now liquefied into curvature of moon
over the Gatineau River, a chalet for one.

Night after night in near orbit,
the ancient heavenly iceberg trails
its gaudy strands of hair, brash
and foreign, paling Polaris, Mars,
familiars to the planet Earth
in the general wobbliness
of space, and time.

On the radio, I hear the comet's
timing is exquisite in California's
southwest skies, shielding a galactic
spaceship from the eyes of the unready.
Chosen Ones lay themselves out,
shed their bodies for the trip, rise
like motes of dust

to fill the hidden vessel
let their real lives begin
vast and unencumbered.

My pitch-black road signals
its own promise, what
we voyagers seem to long for —

a semblance of orderliness in inner space
a chance to give birth to ourselves.

River Ceremonies

Microphones fail and lights blot out
ushering in the quiet fire of candles and a cappella chanting
a riverbank ghat the girls
of Varanasi bring baskets of leaves
cupped around marigolds and candles
to send out on the water

A thousand years ago it could be,
time floats in infinity
on mapped leaves   the sinking weight
of molten wax
drowns moment after moment;
things are too humble to be boundless
but absence stretches out forever.

Here the faithful pray, bathe,
wash clothes and dishes;
pilgrims plunge, the river sickens,
kills with typhoid, polio, jaundice —
the medium of life rife with the offal
of 32 open sewers

                                        Up river
on his funeral pyre, one cadaver's tender feet
lie exposed to flames;
another, still swaddled and garlanded on a litter,
is bathed by his brothers in the holy Ganges —
they have paid wood-sellers
for the pyre piled up and waiting —
his will be the next brief cluster,
one more wavering pool of light.

Liberation

half moon
on its belly
sifts through crushed window panes
fields of Indian marigolds
night train
destination Varanasi
Marnikarnika ghat
gold on Ganges
garlands

Tides On Joggins Beach

Every six hours and thirteen minutes
drowning the beach, leaving it bare
pulled to extremes
pulled to extremes
in the moon's harness

the ardent bay waters.
And the low layered cliffs
sedimentary soft, flush away
on the ebb tide
billions of years.

Ancient pieces of rainforest
litter the sand
for the child's taking
small spines in beach rocks
satin black coal.

He enters raw caves
salvages treasures
from time before thinking when
not even dinosaurs
printed the earth

then leaves for his supper
the beach in a spring tide
inching its way
without hesitation
coldly eroding.

In Medias Res

They couldn't say exactly where the story began
what the starting point was, the kick-off, themselves
in the parking lot waiting for a ferry four hours late

or on the far shore bedding down in a cabin
with a small happy dog, then driving a coastal highway
while winds whipped the Gulf of Saint Lawrence, battered

their straight-sided van heading north.
They used to read books from beginning to end, one at a time
with all the time in the world to sound out long Russian names

recognizing each character along the way
to the flowering of their fate
knowing that was the way it had to be, in the end.

Their own story finds them scrambling over rocks
where the water feels cold at first but then just right
washes over toes while the dog rolls in a decomposing crab.

Here they are: eating fish, watching a play about a shipwreck,
hiking into a landlocked fjord, where they lose and find each other.
On the north shore they follow a path lined with sweet peas

and berry blossoms, the sod huts smoky with verisimilitude,
maybe the Vikings were here, maybe not. Sails
on square-rigged masts stiffening in the blow, they leave shore

wrapped in oilskins, ship out with harbour dolphins
on the unfolding late day sea.

The World According to Maud Lewis

here are safe harbours, seagulls broad as sailboats
the Annapolis Basin,
fairytale farmhouses red on the green hill
yellow barns

here lightly burdened horses in tandem
draw a sleigh over blue-white snow
hoof prints spooling out between runners,
tracing time's arc

what comes to us in dreams
is written in brick-red paint, words for clay
the clarity of childhood
whole straight bodies, yesterday's costumes —

furrows in spring fields, eyelashes on oxen
the dream rises up more real than crookedness and pain;
what we do passes through the screen of who we are
and who's to say what's inconsequential

or more real than our white bus with black letters
that shakes as it ambles up the road
between a deep blue cove   fish barrels on the wharf
and fields of pink and white lady slippers   common wild orchids

Macdonald Gardens (Ottawa, 2002)

> There are cemeteries that are lonely,
> graves full of bones that do not make a sound…
> — Pablo Neruda

There are parks that are lonely
full of empty paths —
maples, old leafy oaks,
endlessly shedding
brown leaves crunching —
then snow, a soggy mass
hardening, narrowing,
the beaten width of two
boot prints.

This city park is built
over graveyards —
old bones plowed under
like china cups with no tea in them.
Death is there
like a bell with no clapper.

No one knows how many
still lie under a park
that shrinks each time diggers
move more earth, builders lay
new foundations. Death resides
in bits of stone mixed
for concrete, wafts its no-smell
to circulate through new halls.
a perfume's soundless
base note under summer flowers.

The park holds its dead like scattered teeth
disremembered.
Children wait for snow
climb the sledding hill —
do not yet recognize lonely Death
in the shrieking rush downhill
tumbling over the near and silent past.

Valparaiso

A teen in a white shirt scrawls today's menu:
mussels and fried fish, tomatoes, avocado
a cavern with dark beams, clean tablecloths
an afternoon meal with Chilean songs

mussels and fried fish, tomato, avocado
in this saliferous port of watch-your-back welcome
an afternoon meal with Chilean songs
then to funiculars scaling the cliffs

in this saliferous port of watch-your-back welcome
three grinning sailors guard the armada
near the funiculars scaling the cliffs
to the poet's house with its view of the harbour

three grinning sailors guard the armada
the Southern Cross high in the deep clear sky
the poet's house with its view of the harbour
hungry renegade dogs bark through the night

the Southern Cross high in the deep clear sky
a cavern with dark beams, clean tablecloths
hungry renegade dogs bark through the night
a teen in a white shirt scrawls today's menu.

Riding the Ocean

the Ocean Limited left the coast last night,
clattered west over tidal bays
rippled with mud flats
Truro, Amherst, Miramichi,
call and response along the rails,
the going and the going back

at the whim of velocity, peaks and valleys
turns in the railbed,
a dance the train leads —
foxtrot, samba, swing gentle enough
to sleep by,
night shades of Amqui, Mont-Joli, Rivière-du-Loup

early August morning fogs the St Lawrence, gauzes
palominos put out to pasture, cows sleep-grazing,
low barns with blue roofs, ripening corn,
ghosts of silver farms advancing, retreating —

the tilt is built into the train
rocking and righting, polished track over curves
a body's sweet suspension
shaken into harmony.

Lowertown: December

In the market a man in a thin
coat no gloves in the minus-eight
afternoon sunshine hands out his poem
praising small kindnesses, *life preservers*
in a sea of despair

Near the hair and tanning salon
police gather a bleeding drunk onto a stretcher
forgive me (how many times has he asked)

In the evening, my host bakes salmon
for the children and me
opens a nice bottle of Italian red

plays his new song, catchy on the porta-studio
breathes out smiles with Thich Nhat Hanh.
Here a fire, a sleepy child, a sleeping cat

outside, the skating rink already gone to sleep
but not the stars
in the dead of winter

The Airing

What is she thinking, this woman with
baby dolls springing up from her breasts
their little heads bobbing over a skimpy
tank top? Fresh from the shower, she wears
an expression remote and dignified.

You have to wonder. It's as though
she's on parade, exhibiting newborns to
the neighbourhood, as though this were a quiet
residential street and she might meet
other mothers who would admire

her plastic newborns, blue eyes open,
a smile on their tiny lips.
But people look and look away,
see a deluded woman on a truck route
where the homeless take shelter.

Does she think, *I am a mother* or, *this show,*
these dolls, this is as close as I get?
Or is there no reason, only the impulse of a little girl
to play house, mixed up with a woman's
sense: what breasts are for.

Tight Blue

> Not every man has gentians in his house
> in soft September, at slow, sad Michaelmas.
> — DH Lawrence

5:30 am. Door slams.
A woman is cursing —
your window open
high above the fence
around the homeless shelter.

She's filthy mad — the details
don't carry as well as
the tight blue curses
their energy punched up
by what she really means to say —

like what am I doing here
why does it have to be so hard
doesn't anyone hear?

If you looked out
you might see her —
small and tough, curly grey hair,
skin darkened by summer,

reach her a blue-forked torch
a cluster of Michaelmas daisies,
Bavarian gentians
for the dark and darker,
the self-guided descent
she's traveling now.

Whiteout (Roundelay for Winter in Eastern Canada, 2006)

the actual thing that overtakes you
crouches where you live —
the likelihood of catastrophe, of snow or rain
          how many trees with deep roots
          remain on the hill, will underground walls
          withstand or crumble

you can be overtaken in different ways
news of the world, the suffering
of shocked survivors

one night on a country road
the snow suddenly thickens
you slow down, low headlights beam
through dancing snow veils
          white road meets white shoulder
          the blanked-out yellow line holds no centre

prelude to tomorrow's thaw, flash freeze
swirling squall
in an hour road sky ditch field
a driven whiteness of cars buses big rigs
indistinguishable shapes
where rescuers grope, sirens muffled

                    37 vehicles, 4 dead, 40 injured

the actual thing that overtakes you
is born the same place you are
here a whiteout
there a mudslide   somewhere else a mine collapses

Hunter's Moon

for Patti Irwin (1942-2008)

Klieg lights burn the middle of the road,
switch on midnight bright as an operating theatre —
street surgeons see where to cut, dig,
fill in. You can draw the curtains but there's
no stopping the grind, rumble, crash, beep,
no quick-fix clearing of temporary closures.
Stone cold moon adds its sanguine beams:
no place to hide, the forecast is for blood.

What do the diggers discover, then cover
up for paving over, patching the roadbed?
If cancer struck beneath streets,
deep in the earth, drills and backhoes
could still extricate every renegade morsel,
even under this moon. A road would carry on.

Black Pot

Today in the forest we take a wrong turn
a house tucked between rustling trees
in the back an old iron pot
insists we look into its discarded depths.

It's Baba Yaga's pot, asking why
we've come, waiting for our wrong
answers so it can boil us alive —
wrong answers our hearts know

are deceitful. We back away, mouths numb
in the depths of our ignorance.
The pot lets us go, its cackles
fading on the same wind that shuffles trees,

warm dry leaves nearly bursting into flame.
We have not lost our way for nothing.

Yellow Calls Us to the Things of the World

Lemon slickers, golden arches,
ochred calendula. Raw-siennad
oak leaves. Yellow yields.
Mediates between stop and go.

Makes school buses visible.
Paints straight lines down the middle
of black asphalt to keep the world
right. In deciduous maturity,

yellow releases the tree
from its green youth, lets go
minor gods of luminescence:
wait, it says. Wait. Look.

Notes

Instructions for the Era of Water — according to a news report, “The Dutch are gearing up for climate change with the construction of floating houses.”

Constellation — epigraph is from “Scar Tissue” by Charles Wright.

Ice Fog — epigraph is from “Sunday Morning” by Wallace Stevens.

Selene is a moon goddess in Greek mythology.

Call of the Wild is for Danny.

Black Umbrellas/Nunc Stans — the line, thunderstorms light us and roll on by, is from “The Silent Generation II” by Charles Wright. Nunc stans is variously translated as the eternal now, “eternity as the standing still of the present time” (Aquinas), “a widespread now in which [a human] spends his life” (Hannah Arendt, *The Life of the Mind*).

Equilibrium — the line, Glory be to God for dappled things, is from the poem “Pied Beauty” by Gerard Manley Hopkins.

The Medici Princess is after a box construction by Joseph Cornell.

Percy’s Remains — epigraph is from “Of Modern Poetry” by Wallace Stevens.

Fifteen — “the Boston States” was (is?) commonly used in Nova Scotia to mean New England.

February — epigraph is from “Cold Mountain Poems” by Han Shan, hermit and poet of the Tang Dynasty (translated by Gary Snyder).

Aunt Tango — epigraph is from *The Beauty of the Husband* by Anne Carson (cover flap).

The Weight of Snow — epigraph is from “A Piece of The Storm” by Mark Strand.

The World According to Maud Lewis — Maud Lewis (1903-1970) was a folk artist who lived in the Digby area of Nova Scotia and sold her art from her little house beside the road.

Macdonald Gardens (Ottawa, 2002) — epigraph is from Neruda’s “Nothing but Death” (translated by Robert Bly). This park in Ottawa’s Lowertown was once a consecrated burying ground then reborn as a park with the remains of many unclaimed bodies plowed under.

Tight Blue — epigraph is from “Bavarian Gentians” by D.H. Lawrence.

Hunter’s Moon — October’s full moon is called “hunter’s moon” or sometimes “blood moon” after hunters who tracked and killed their prey by autumn moonlight.

Yellow Calls Us to the Things of the World is after Richard Wilber’s poem “Love Calls Us to the Things of the World.”

Eco-Audit
Printing this book using Rolland Enviro 100 Print instead of virgin fibres paper saved the following resources:

Trees	Solid Waste	Water	Air Emissions	Natural Gas
2	67 kg	6,304 L	146 kg	10 m^3